Terrifying Tudors

Terry Deary

Illustrated by **Martin Brown**

This book is dedicated to all the readers around the world who have made Horrible Histories such a success

Text © Terry Deary, 1998, 2013
Illustrations © Martin Brown, 1998, 2013
Cover line and colour by Rob Davis, 2018
Index by Caroline Hamilton

ISBN 978 1407 17853 0

Printed and bound in the UK by CPI Group (UK) Ltd, Croydon, CR0 4YY

2 4 6 8 10 9 7 5 3 1

The right of Terry Deary and Martin Brown to be identified as the author and illustrator of this work respectively has been asserted by them in accordance with the Copyright, Designs and Patents Act, 1988.

Papers used by Scholastic Children's Books are made from wood grown in sustainable forests.

www.scholastic.co.uk

Contents

Introduction

History can be horrible. And who made it horrible? The vicious and cruel people who lived in the past.

And here's an amazing thing ... some of the most horrible people in history all had names beginning with the letter 'T'. Just look in your little sister's copy of Tiddly Tots' Alphabet of Terrors.

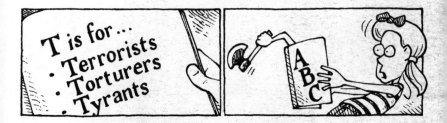

Or ask your teacher...

And the Tudors were truly terrifying torturing tyrants. Even worse than teachers!

6

The first Tudor had the bloodstained body of his defeated enemy tied to a horse and shown to the people. The message was clear…

The last Tudor had her boyfriend beheaded on a bloody block.

And, in between, there were thousands of people hanged, burned, boiled and chopped just to keep the Tudors on top.

This book is full of **foul facts** and **savage stories** about the fun-loving Tudor family and their suffering subjects. Terrifying Tudors in fact. It would bring tears to the eyes of Tyrannosaurus rex. It may scare you witless, so be warned ... do not read this book with the lights out!

Henry the Mean Monarch

1485

Richard III is hacked to death at the Battle of Bosworth Field. His opponent, Henry Tudor, is crowned **Henry VII**. This man is ruthless … and quite toothless too … but not uthless when it comes to money. He makes England rich.

1509

Henry VII dies. All that money didn't do him much good. Never mind, his son, **Henry VIII**, will spend it for him on wine, women and wars.

King Henry VII
(reigned 1485–1509)

In 1485 England was ruled by the last of the Plantagenet kings, **Richard III.** Richard was a hard-hearted man – he probably had his brother's children **suffocated** in the Tower of London.

THERE'S NOTHING WRONG WITH THAT, IS THERE? YOUNG EDWARD WAS JUST 12 YEARS OLD WHEN HE WAS SMOTHERED. SO HIS HEAD WOULD HAVE BEEN A BIT SMALL FOR THE CROWN ANYWAY

WEAK KINGS ONLY CAUSE TROUBLE AS STRONG LORDS SQUABBLE TO CONTROL THE COUNTRY. IMAGINE WHAT WOULD HAPPEN IF YOU HAD A 12-YEAR-OLD TEACHER FOR YOUR CLASS? CHAOS!

Ruthless Richard had his enemies – most kings did in those days. Those enemies looked around for someone to take Richard III's place.

There were 12 people in line to the throne but none could hope to beat Richard in battle. So Richard's enemies turned to the 13th in line to the throne – an almost unknown Welshman called Henry Tudor.

Henry landed in Wales with a small force and marched east. Richard gathered his army and marched west. They met in the middle and fought the Battle of Bosworth Field in Leicestershire. Richard's friends deserted him and went over to Henry Tudor's side.

Suddenly England had a Tudor king, Henry VII, and no one was as surprised as Henry. Then the battle began to hold on to his throne.

There were plenty of 'pretenders' who said they should be king, but only one got really close to stopping the Tudors in their tracks. A boy called Lambert Simnel said he was one of the princes in the Tower. His Uncle Richard had NOT murdered him. Lambert was King not Henry Tudor.

Henry Tudor went into battle with little Lambert and won (the battle of Stoke). Did Henry hack the head of Lambert? No! He gave the lad a job in the palace kitchen.

Lambert Simnel became a faithful servant to Henry VII and, in time, was promoted to become the falconer to Henry VII's son, King Henry VIII. He was still alive 40 years after the battle against Henry Tudor.

Neither Henry VII nor any other English king rode out to face rebels on a battlefield again. A second pretender, Perkin Warbeck, tried to invade from Scotland but failed. Again Henry Tudor treated him with mercy. But foolish Warbeck kept plotting and Henry had to act. Warbeck was executed, along with the real Earl of Warwick, in 1499.

❝DID YOU KNOW?
HENRY TUDOR WAS ALWAYS CONSIDERED
TO BE A 'LUCKY' KING AND HE USED THIS
LUCK TO ARGUE, 'GOD IS ON MY SIDE.'
AFTER THE BATTLE OF STOKE, FOR
EXAMPLE, NEWS GOT BACK TO LONDON
THAT HENRY HAD BEEN DEFEATED. A
SUPPORTER OF LAMBERT SIMNEL,
JOHN SWIT, STOOD UP AND
MADE A SPEECH,
CLAIMING THAT HENRY
TUDOR HAD GOT THE DEATH HE
DESERVED. THEN, BEFORE
HE FINISHED SPEAKING,
JOHN SWIT'S FACE SEEMED
TO TURN PURPLE AND THEN
BLACK AND HE DROPPED DOWN
DEAD! HENRY TUDOR WAS
AMUSED.❞

The crafty king

Henry Tudor was 'careful' with his money. The gossips in the palace said the Queen wore buckles of tin because the King was too mean to buy her silver. Her gowns were mended time and time again, frayed cuffs turned up and worn threads patched. They also said she had to borrow money from her servants.

But Henry was just as careful with his country's money as he was with his own. When the pretender, Perkin Warbeck, led an army to attack the country, Henry Tudor had to raise an army too. That cost money. The soldiers had to have weapons and food and they had to be fed.

Warbeck's army was defeated and Henry captured the rebel lords. He could have had them executed. Instead he fined them and let them go home to raise the money.

The bills for Henry's army came to £13,200, which would be worth over a million pounds today. But the lords paid him £14,700 in fines. So, Henry VII managed to make a £1,500 profit out of being attacked. That's crafty.

Horrible Henry

1509

Henry VIII takes the throne because his older brother, Arthur, has carelessly died. Big Hen not only takes Arthur's crown but his wife, Catherine, too. Henry loves **sport, fighting, music and eating**. Most of all he loves himself.

1536

Henry decides he wants rid of his old wife Cathy … so he puts himself in charge of the Church and grants himself a divorce. The old Catholic Church and its monks and monasteries are banned. Big Hen pockets their wealth, of course. And, of course, **rebels get the chop**. Soon he starts chopping wives, too (Anne Boleyn and Catherine Howard) and divorcing wives (Catherine of Aragon and Anne of Cleves). Favourite wife, Jane, dies giving birth to their son, Edward ... who'll become the next Tudor king.

1547

Mad, bad Henry VIII dies (which saves a lot on the palace food bills). He leaves England poorer and divided, and sickly, nine-year-old Edward VI, in charge. Sad.

King Henry VIII
(reigned 1509–1547)

Henry wasn't ruler of England because he was wise, strong and just. He was king because his father, Henry VII, had been king and his older brother, Arthur, had died.

Of course, if anyone had said in Tudor times that Henry was mad they'd have been playing football with their own head.

Henry reigned for 38 torturing Tudor years and, in that time, up to 72,000 people were executed. That's about 1,900 a year, or five every day. It must have been a bit like a National Lottery with 35 losers every week.

Take a look at these topped Tudor victims…

Lottery of life losers
Margaret Pole,
Countess of Salisbury – 1541

What would you do if an executioner said…

RIGHT MATE, LET'S HAVE YOUR NECK ON THIS CHOPPING BLOCK

Would you do as you were told? Would you say, as you were supposed to, 'I forgive you, executioner,' and give him a bag of gold? Or would you be really rotten to the poor axeman, like the eccentric old Countess of Salisbury?

Henry VIII planned to visit York. He wanted the Tower of London empty of prisoners so none would escape while his back was turned. One of those prisoners was the Countess of Salisbury. When it was her turn to be executed, Henry's chief executioner, Master Cratwell, was away from London. The job was left to a boy. You have to feel sorry for him!

If the young executioner had written a letter home then it might have looked something like this…

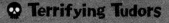

Tower Green
London
1541

Dear Mum,
  Started my new job as
executioner today. It's not as
easy as it looks! I have a nice
uniform. Here's a
picture I drew
looking in a
mirror:

You'd be proud of me — except you wouldn't know it was me 'cos Henry's executioners are ~~anommynus annunnymous~~ secret.

Anyway, the boss, Robert Cratwell (whose name I can't tell you 'cos it's secret), said I could start with an easy one. 'It's the old Countess of Salisbury,' he said. 'She's nearly 70 years old so she'll be no trouble.'

'Seventy!' I said. 'If she gets any older her head'll probably just drop off!' I laughed. I didn't know the joke would be on me! 'What's the old trout done?' I asked.

'Nothing,' Robert said. 'She's never had a trial or been found guilty. But her son, Cardinal Pole, was a Catholic and he started stirring up trouble for the King. So Henry had the Cardinal's old mother thrown in the Tower a couple of years ago. And the King made sure she suffered in there with terrible food and no heating. The old woman will be glad to be out of it.'

Then he gave me a few last-minute lessons in chopping and sent me off to do some target practice on a turnip. I was spot on. That turnip was sliced as neat as one that you'd put in your stew, Mum. But there was no one watching, was there? And turnips don't move.

Imagine the shock when I found dozens of people gathered round the scaffold! I was shaking with nerves, I can tell you. 'Would you mind putting your head on the block?' I asked her, ever so polite, just the way you taught me.

Blow me, but the old woman said, 'No! A traitor would put their head on the block, but I'm not a traitor, so I won't!'

Her two guards grabbed her and held her down on her knees. But she was struggling all the time. They couldn't hold her head down because I'd have cut their hands off. That meant she could still move her head around. Then she looked up at me and said, 'Catch me if you can.' She started bobbing and weaving and I started chopping. Well, I made a right mess of her shoulders before I finally got her in the neck and finished her off.

It was my job to hold up the head and cry, 'Behold the head of a traitor!' I was that scared I think I said, 'Behold the head of a tater!' The witnesses were booing and throwing things at me. It was awful, Mum.

But Robert's back now and I'm getting extra lessons. In the meantime I'm working away in the torture chamber. They don't mind if you're clumsy in there and you don't have a big audience.

Give my love to the kids and the cat. I'll be home next week to help with chopping the firewood. Love,

Your little Georgie

We don't know what happened to the boy executioner – but his master, Cratwell, was later hanged for robbery!

Of course the good news is that Henry VIII died of a slow disease. His legs had ulcers – open sores that had to be bandaged to stop them dripping all over the place. The Countess of Salisbury's death was messy ...
but Henry's was long, slow and painful. It's hard to feel sorry for him.

Cardinal John Fisher – June 1535

If you had the power of a king, would you send your dear old teacher for the chop? (On second thoughts, you'd better not answer that!)

HenryVIII's old teacher was called John Fisher. Henry's mother had put Prince Henry in Fisher's special care. But, when the old teacher disagreed with Henry's plans for the Church, Henry ordered the old man's imprisonment.

Some prisoners lived in comfort, but John Fisher spent winter in the Tower of London with just a handful of rags to cover him. In spring, just when he was beginning to warm up, Henry ordered his teacher's death. When Fisher walked to the block he staggered because he was so weak from hunger.

Still, witnesses said he was eager to meet his

death and he dressed for what he described as his 'wedding day'.

The Pope had made Fisher a 'cardinal' while the old man was in prison. Henry was furious…

I will send your head to Rome so the Pope can put your cardinal's hat on you himself.

Henry never carried out that threat.

Fisher didn't give the executioner any trouble, but his body was left almost naked for a whole day while the head was stuck on a spike over London Bridge.

Spanish visitors said the heads of traitors over the bridge turned black but Fisher's stayed fresh – this proved he was a saint, they said. It would be interesting to see if it was still fresh today, but you can't. Not only is the old London Bridge gone, but a friend of Fisher's climbed up to the top of the bridge tower one night to pinch the head and give it a proper burial.

Fisher was 66 years old. He was hardly a Tudor terrorist who needed putting to death for Henry's safety.

The Carthusian monks – May 1535

A 'terrorist' is someone who tries to terrify people into doing what they want. So Henry VIII was a terrorist. It wasn't enough to have his enemies locked away or even executed. He had to make an example of them.

Three monks from the Carthusian order opposed Henry and were sentenced to be drawn, hanged and quartered. [1]

That is, drawn feet-first to the scaffold on a sledge,

1 Some historians describe this punishment for treason as 'hung, drawn and quartered' where 'drawn' means having the bowels drawn from the body. Not that you'd be too worried about getting the words right if it happened to you!

hanged till half-dead,

ARE YOU FAMILIAR WITH THE WORD "OVERKILL"?

taken down and cut open so their guts could be burned on a fire, then beheaded and quartered.

Then, to strike terror into the hearts of their supporters, the severed arm of one monk was nailed to the door of his monastery.

Another Carthusian, Sebastian Newdigate, had been a friend of Henry's and they'd gone hunting together. Henry made an example of him by placing him in a London street, loaded down with chains and lead weights so he couldn't move or even stand up. (Worse … he couldn't go to the toilet!) He was left, in his own filth, with no food or water until he died. The message was as clear as ever…

Anne Boleyn – 1536

All the school history books will tell you that Henry had wanted a divorce from his first wife, Catherine of Aragon. When the Catholic Church refused to give him a divorce, he scrapped the Catholic Church, made his own church and gave himself a divorce.

Catholics who objected were ruthlessly punished. Even Catherine and Henry's own daughter, Mary Tudor, was locked up for protesting. (New wife Anne didn't like Mary much anyway.) And all for what? Nothing! Because the divorce was pointless when Catherine of Aragon died in 1536 anyway. (There are stories that Anne Boleyn had Catherine poisoned with a delivery of Welsh beer to her castle-prison. That's unlikely.)

One of Henry's best friends, Sir Thomas More, was executed for sticking to his Catholic religion. But, before he died, he said something very wise…

Anne Boleyn might strike our heads off like footballs, but it won't be long before her head will dance the same dance!

(It makes you wonder where Thomas More had ever seen a dancing football, but that's beside the point.)

More was right. Henry grew fed up with Anne when she failed to give him a son. He had her executed for flirting with other men.

What the school history books don't tell you is how kind old Henry was when it came to Anne's execution. He didn't want any of that hacking about and sawing at necks. He sent for a real expert. A swordsman.

Anne Boleyn never laid her neck on a block. She walked onto the scaffold, said a few words of farewell and was blindfolded. The swordsman didn't want her turned towards him so he said…

Clean off, first time. (Unlike a French swordsman, who took 29 swings of the sword to execute the Count of Chalais in 1626!)

SWISH!(24)

SNICK

I THINK HIS HOOD'S ON BACK TO FRONT

Hundreds of years later there were ghost stories of Anne wandering round the Tower with her head tucked underneath her arm. But there were different ghost stories told at the time of the execution. They said...

• Candles around the tomb of Catherine of Aragon, Anne's enemy, burst into flame the day before the execution. As the blow fell on Anne's neck the next day, the candles went out just as mysteriously. (It could have been the draught from the sword! But, as Catherine was buried 92 miles away in Peterborough, it's a bit unlikely.)

• As Anne died, people reported seeing hares running across the fields – a hare was the sign of a witch, and Anne was suspected of witchcraft. Every year, on the anniversary of the execution on 19 May, hares were seen. Perhaps they still are!

Robert Aske – 1537

In 1536, Henry VIII had created his Church of England but not everyone was happy. In fact, some were ready to revolt.

The changes were unpopular, especially in the north of England which had never been too keen on taking orders from rulers in the south.

Riots broke out in Lincoln. Henry had a bit of a problem because he had no army ready to crush the riots. Eventually the Duke of Suffolk raised an army and the Lincoln rebels began to go home.

But a new protest, led by the very religious Catholic, Robert Aske, broke out in Pontefract in the north. (Aske had only one eye. Is this why he didn't see eye to eye with Henry?) Aske's protestors called themselves the 'Pilgrimage of Grace'.

These pilgrims carried banners and wore badges that showed the bleeding wounds of Christ – but they weren't bloodthirsty. In fact they were ordinary men and women who wanted to make a peaceful protest.

The Duke of Suffolk had no men to spare to attack Aske because he was too busy in Lincoln. Henry was in desperate trouble.

Only one man could save Henry! And he did. That man was ... Robert Aske! Aske said he was not a rebel and he didn't want to destroy Henry. He made his own declaration...

The Pilgrimage of Grace

We are not going on our Pilgrimage of Grace for earthly gains.
We are doing it...

- for the love of Almighty God
- for his true Catholic Church
- and for the future of that church

We wish to do this by...

- preserving King Henry and his family
- by driving out all wicked lords
- sacking the king's evil ministers

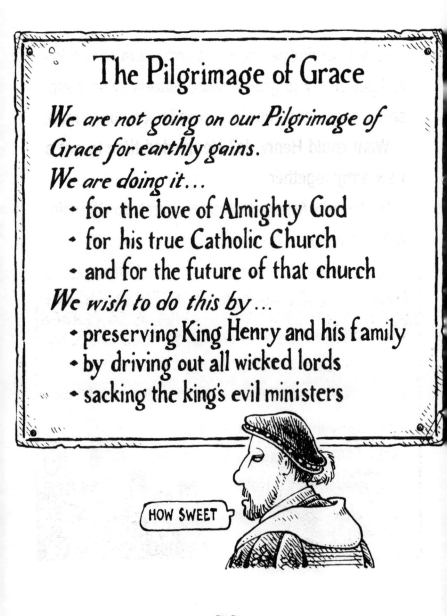

HOW SWEET

Aske's pilgrims wanted to march south to London to force Henry to give in. Aske refused to let them, saying they were a holy group and not a rioting mob.

What could Henry do? He needed time to get a new army together.

So he told Aske a whopping great fib. He said, more or less…

Then he gathered his forces. Some peasants in Cumberland marched on Carlisle and said they were part of the 'Pilgrimage of Grace' (though they weren't). That was just the excuse Henry had been waiting for.

Henry sent in his new army and attacked ruthlessly. Places like Sawley monastery had been reopened by the Pilgrims – Henry's men took the monks and hanged them from the steeple of the church so everyone could see what happened to rebels.

Aske was executed in front of the people who had followed him. Hundreds of his supporters were hanged and a woman was even burned.

So much for Henry's promises.

THAT'S WHAT YOU GET WHEN YOU TAKE ON A TUDOR!

"DID YOU KNOW?
IT WAS AGAINST THE LAW TO
FORETELL THE DEATH OF A MONARCH.
ANYONE WHO SAID, 'THE KING IS GOING
TO DIE,' WOULD BE EXECUTED.
HENRY VIII FELL ILL WITH A FEVER
IN 1547 AND HIS DOCTORS KNEW HE WAS
GOING TO DIE. BUT THEY
DIDN'T DARE TELL HIM
HE WAS GOING TO DIE
BECAUSE THEY'D HAVE
BEEN BREAKING THE LAW
AND THEY COULD HAVE
BEEN HANGED!
SO HENRY SLIPPED OFF TO
SLEEP, THINKING HE WAS
GOING TO LIVE. HE MUST HAVE
BEEN REALLY DISAPPOINTED
WHEN HE WOKE UP DEAD.

HE WAS 55 YEARS OLD AND
THE THRONE PASSED TO HIS
NINE-YEAR-OLD SON EDWARD VI.
(THE PRETENDER, LAMBERT SIMNEL, HAD
BEEN CROWNED EDWARD VI 60 YEARS
BEFORE. SO HENRY'S
SON WAS REALLY EDWARD THE SIXTH
THE SECOND.)**"**

Fat Hen

Henry VIII is famous for his huge feasts and his belt-busting eating habits. But what do you know about the Tudors and their tastes? Try this quick quiz and strain your brain! (Or challenge your friends to a competition – see who can score the most – but don't forget to cheat and look at the answers. After all, this is a Horrible Histories book and it is not suitable for honest, fair and truthful readers.)

1 What would Tudor magistrates do with a merchant who added sawdust to his peppers and spices?

a Make him eat a plate filled with the spicy-sawdust mix.

FOLLOWED BY A LITTLE CURRIED PLANK PERHAPS

b Lock his head in a pillory and burn the spices under his nose.

c Let him starve till he has picked out every bit of sawdust from the spice powder.

I GUESS THIS MAKES ME A WOODPICKER

SPICE

2 In 1502, the first European to taste chocolate hated it. Who was it?

a Christopher Columbus.

b Henry VIII (when he was an 11-year-old prince).

c Henry VII's pet dog who pinched it from the palace kitchen and was sick.

3 In 1500, the first cookery book was published in the English language. What was it called?

a The Two Fat Lardies

b Filling Feasts for 1500

c The Boke of Cokery

4 Pork and chicken could be served together. How?

a The back half of a cooked pig was sewn onto the front half of a cockerel.

b Pork and chicken were minced together into 'chork sausages'.

c A pig was fed on chicken meat, killed, cooked and served.

SERVES YOU RIGHT!

5 Kitchen workers in great houses got special treats to add to their wages. Which of the following was often included?

a Leftover food.

b Sheep's eyes to take home for their family suppers.

c Grease scraped from the bottom of the pot when meat has been boiled.

6 Beer was often warmed up and drunk with what dropped in?

a Frog-spawn.

b Toast.

c A silver coin for luck.

7 King Henry VIII treated his wife, Catherine of Aragon, cruelly by giving her a gift of what?

a Old wine.

b New wine.

c A cup of tea.

8 How would you have eaten 'stockfish' in Tudor times?

a Skinned, gutted and eaten raw.

b Battered with chips.

c Battered with a hammer.

9 Who was the 'Queen of the Pea'?

a The lavatory cleaner.

b Anne Boleyn because she had pea-green sleeves.

c A woman who found a pea in her Christmas cake.

I WEAR THEM FOR HENRY. HE'S OBSESSED BY GREEN SLEEVES. COMPLETELY NUTS. HE'S EVEN WRITTEN A SONG ABOUT THE THINGS!

10 How would Henry VIII have eaten his meat?

a Carved a piece from the bone, dipped it in a sauce and put it in his mouth.

b Chewed the meat from the bone and thrown the bone to his dogs.

c Torn the meat with his bare hands, stuffed it in his mouth and wiped his hands on his tunic.

Answers

1b In 1493 the London Grocers' Company employed men whose job it was to check spices as they came into the port. Merchants had been adding gravel to peppercorns and nutmeg and other spices. These checkers were known as 'garbellers' – not to be confused with history teachers who rush through lessons. They are garblers, but they probably won't set fire to pepper under your nose.

2a Columbus had discovered America in 1492. Ten years later he was visiting the Gulf of Honduras when natives offered him a drink of xocoatl (pronounced chocoatl). It was mixed with honey and spices and served cold and frosty. Columbus drank it politely but said, 'Yeuch!' Still, he brought some beans back to Europe and now it's a billion-pound industry. Hands up if you thought chocolate bars came from Mars?

3c 'Cokery' was just the Tudor way of writing cookery – it had nothing to do with drinking the fizzy drink … or eating lumps of coke for that matter. Don't you learn some amazing things from this boke?

BLIMEY!
DOES THAT MEAN
US BLOKES ARE
REALLY BLOOKS?

4a Cooks often sewed two creatures together to make an entertaining meal. The front of a chicken and back of a pig stitched together made the legendary creature, the 'cockatrice'. They also served a pig's stomach stuffed with minced pork and spices, then covered with almonds to look like a hedgehog. (If you're really stupid you could sew the front of a jeep on to the back of a dog to try to get a Land Rover.) Vegetables were also carved into fantastic shapes of birds and animals. Would you enjoy a carrot parrot?

Baked potumpkin

5c You too could have some nice grease if you worked hard. You may also get rabbit skins (after the angry rabbits had been cooked and became hot cross bunnies). You could also have free clothes and good shoes. But you couldn't have leftover food scraps. They had to be given to the poor. But if a joint of meat or a pie had not been touched then it belonged to the person who served it!

I DON'T WANT TO PUT YOU OFF, M'LADY, BUT THAT PIE'S NOT VERY NICE

6b Warm beer with toast dropped in! Urgh! But it was better than some of the other things stirred in to give it a bit of flavour … like raw egg! And a popular Tudor Christmas drink (that you may like to leave for Santa Claus instead of a glass of sherry) was called 'lambswool'. This was hot beer with roasted apple pieces, nutmeg, ginger and sugar. When it was whipped up, the scum (sorry, froth) on the top looked like lambs' wool.

7b Catherine was ill and wanted some old Spanish wine to soothe her aches. Henry ordered new wine to be sent to her – in Tudor times this would make a sick person worse, and Fat Hen knew this. A kind servant sent Catherine the old wine that she wanted. When Henry found out, the servant was sacked. The old wine gift had given Henry a new whine.

8c Stockfish was dried fish and it was hard as a history teacher's heart! You had to batter it with a wooden hammer and soak it in water for two hours before you could chew it. So strike a pike, clout a trout, pound a flounder or bludgeon a gudgeon … but be careful not to get flat fishy fingers.

9c On the 12th night after Christmas (6 January if you haven't got a calendar) many houses celebrated by baking a fruit cake. A pea (or a bean) was baked into the cake. The person who found it became the King or Queen of the Pea (or Bean). They sat at the head of the table and got the best food, but had to entertain all the guests.

10a Shocking but true. Henry is often pictured as eating like an animal with grease dripping down his beard and servants ducking the bare bones as he threw them over his shoulder. But he was a great prince who would eat in the correct Tudor manner: carved pieces of meat dipped in sauces and placed in the mouth. Cats and dogs were banned from the dining rooms and clothes were far too fine and expensive to have greasy hands wiped over them. Hands would be washed in rose water and dried on linen napkins. Of course, Henry ate huge amounts, but he didn't have the manners of a pig as most people seem to think. (He'd have been shocked to see the average school dinner hall at lunchtime!)

Little Ed

1547

Edward VI, Tudor the third, takes the throne. He is a Catholic-hating young man. He is also God-fearing, which is just as well because he'll be meeting him soon.

1553

Weedy Ed dies at the age of 15. It's party time for the Catholics. **No more Tudor kings ... ever!**

King Edward VI
(reigned 1547–1553)

Henry VIII had waited 28 years for a son and at last Edward was born. Ed's mother, Jane Seymour, died after giving birth, which was very thoughtless of her. Henry wasn't going to lose baby Ed, so he tried to make sure he was properly cared for. If cotton wool had been invented then, Henry would have wrapped his son in the stuff.

Did you know?

1 The floors and walls of Edward's rooms were washed down three times every day to keep him free from disease. No wonder he grew up a bit wet!

WELL, HE'S NOT SICK BUT HE IS A BIT MOULDY

2 Although Edward was precious to his father, Henry hardly ever visited him or read the reports the servants sent him.

3 Edward was raised by nurses because his mother died when he was just a few days old. But his chief nurse was called 'Mother Jack'. That must have confused him a bit. But it is no excuse for the ancient historical joke…

4 Edward took everything very seriously. His teachers thought he was wonderful and very good at history. The trouble was he had no sense of humour. It was reported that he only laughed out loud once in his life! Maybe his teachers should have given him a Horrible Histories book to read!

5 King Henry sent the sons of his favourite lords to do lessons with Edward so the boy wouldn't grow up alone. But it was a dangerous job being a schoolmate of Little Ed. Once Edward's friends persuaded him to swear 'thunderous oaths' like Henry VIII. Edward did this and was told off. But his friends were given a whipping.

6 Little Ed may have grown up to be a Big Ed … and almost certainly a big-head too! His teacher, John Cheke, fell ill. Edward told everyone, 'He will be all right. This morning I prayed for him and God will answer my prayer.' Would you pray for your teacher to get better?

7 Edward also had his father's terrible Tudor cruelty. In a fit of temper he once took a falcon and pulled out all its feathers one by one. He then ripped it into four pieces and threatened that he would do the same to his teachers. (Teachers probably deserve to be torn into four pieces ... but you wouldn't hurt a poor little falcon, would you?)

8 Edward died a painful death from a lung disease known as 'consumption'. The Duke of Northumberland was Edward's protector (a protector ran the country when the monarch was too young to do it). He wanted to keep Ed alive as long as possible – or long enough for Ed to change his will and name Lady Jane Grey as the next queen. So Northumberland sacked Edward's doctors and employed a 'wise woman'. The special potion she fed the dying King contained the poison arsenic. It kept him alive

… but in agony at the same time. Ed was in so much pain he was praying to God to let him kick the bucket. Once Ed had changed his will, Northumberland was ready to let Edward die. The protector sacked the wise woman and called the royal doctors back. There is even a story that Northumberland had the wise woman murdered. But that's daft. If she was a wise woman she'd have seen it coming and escaped!

9 The people of London heard that Edward was dead – or dying. They marched to Greenwich Palace and said…

Edward's attendants knew the dying King was too weak to go out and meet them so they said…

So Northumberland ordered the attendants to lift Ed out of bed, carry him to the window and prop him up so the people could see their king. The plan didn't work all that well because the people were shocked by what they saw. Ed's skinny body was swollen, his fingers were turning black and dropping off. His hair had fallen out. He looked like something the attendants had dug out of the graveyard.

10 The common people were sure that Northumberland was trying to poison Edward. (Which he was!) Northumberland said it was Mary Tudor's fault. He said that last time Mary visited her brother she cast an evil spell over him...

She overlooked him with the evil eye of witchcraft!

Mary was popular at that time. No one believed Northumberland. He was going to be in trouble if Mary ever took the throne.

Daft doctors

Edward VI's doctors made one last attempt to save Ed's life. If you ever get consumption like Little Ed then take antibiotics – or take a plastic bag to collect your fingers and toes when they drop off – but do not take what Ed's doctors gave him…

For consumption

You will need:

Nine teaspoons of spearmint syrup
Turnip
Dates
Raisins
Celery
Pork from a nine-day-old sow

Method:

Grind the dry ingredients together and
stir into the syrup.
Feed to the patient until he is cured.

Footnote: If the patient cannot swallow
the potion then he may well be dead.

No wonder Edward VI's minister, William Cecil, said…

> *God protect us from doctors.*

Just to add a final gruesome touch to Ed's death, a sudden summer storm sprang up. Lightning flashed, thunder crashed … and hailstones as red as fresh blood rained down. 'Henry VIII wanted Mary to be queen,' the people said. 'Northumberland is trying to get Lady Jane Grey on the throne. Henry has risen from the grave! This storm has been sent by Henry to show his anger!'

Ed died.

The curious case of the corpse

Edward VI's grave is in Westminster Abbey. But is his body buried there? There is a strange story that dead Ed was not the corpse in the coffin.

Here is a story that you may or may not believe…

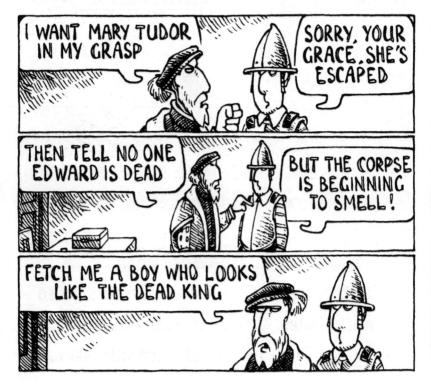

Northumberland's servants found a young man who looked a bit like Edward…

So, the story goes, a substitute corpse is buried in Westminster Abbey. The real Edward VI is somewhere in the grounds of Greenwich Palace.

Is this gory story true? Here's a clue.

The body that was supposed to be Edward's was preserved, laid in an open coffin and taken to the Abbey. Twelve lords took it in turns to guard the coffin before the day of the funeral. This was quite usual.

BUT ... a shocked visitor from France wrote that the 12 lords watched over the coffin 'without torches or tapers'.

Imagine that – babysitting a corpse in the dark!

Why? Work it out for yourself.

The kiss of death

Edward was still just 15 when he fell seriously ill so the country was controlled by a 'protector', the Duke of Northumberland. The Duke had a great idea…

YOU CAN'T LEAVE THE CROWN TO YOUR CATHOLIC SISTER MARY -YOU HATE CATHOLICS. WHY NOT LEAVE IT TO LADY JANE GREY-SHE'S A GOOD PROTESTANT

LADY JANE IS MARRIED TO YOUR SON, ISN'T SHE?

OH! SILLY ME! I'D FORGOTTEN! NEVER MIND, SHE'LL MAKE A GREAT QUEEN

Ed died and Jane was proclaimed queen. Angry Mary marched in and had her arrested. Jane was queen for just nine days and was arrested when she was just 15 years old. She saw her 16th birthday ... but not her 17th. Mary had her executed.

Edward VI left Jane Grey the crown though she never got to wear it. It would have been kinder if he'd left her a bottle of his poisonous medicine.

Misery Mary

1553

Mary I, Tudor four, takes the throne. She's even more miserable than little brother Ed was. She is also a devout Catholic. The English people don't know if they're coming or going with this religious yo-yo.

1554

Mary marries **King Philip of Spain**. She marries for love, he marries to get his paws on the English crown. When he doesn't get it, he goes home in a huff. He'll be back ... with a few thousand troops and an armada.

1558

Now Mary dies. She's lasted even less time than little brother Ed! Three Tudor funerals in 11 years and the family are hopping the twig like budgerigars. New Protestant queen, Mary's half-sister Elizabeth, will stay on her royal perch a lot longer.

Queen Mary I
(reigned 1553–1558)

Mary was a misery. Her dad had divorced her mum, Catherine of Aragon, to marry Anne Boleyn. When Mary tried to fight for Catherine, Henry had her shut up in some miserable and uncomfortable houses. But, before he died, he said Mary could be queen if Edward died without children.

Of course Edward did die. But Ed's chief minister, the Duke of Northumberland, wasn't going to give up his power that easily. He plonked little Jane Grey on the throne, put one of his sons on the throne beside her and sent another of his sons to capture Mary.

Mary knew the English people would not be happy with a Catholic queen. When some Protestants from Cambridge found that she had spent the night in a nearby house they burned the house down!

So how could Mary win the support of the Protestants?

a Tell the English they would be Catholic whether they liked it or not.

b Give up her Catholic religion.

c Lie. Tell the English the country would stay Protestant then change it when she became queen.

c Of course. She was a Tudor, after all, and 'Fibber' was her middle name. Mary said...

The religion of England will not change very much from my brother's reign.

It worked. (The Tudor people hadn't yet learned the lesson, 'Never trust a Tudor.') Gentlemen and peasants made an army of 15,000 to march on London in support of Mary. The Duke of Northumberland marched out to meet Mary's army. And what did the Londoners do as soon as Northumberland left? Rebelled, of course, and offered their support to Mary.

In London they celebrated by...

They were pleased. They sent a letter to Mary that said…

> *Dear Mary Your Grace*
>
> *Your loyal people of London want you to know that we are right behind you. We always have been but, while Northumberland was here, we had to keep quiet to prevent innocent blood being shed*
>
> *Your loyal council*

Ho! Ho! A likely story. But Mary was happy enough to accept their offer of support.

Even little Jane Grey said she was happy. She said…

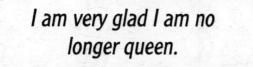

I am very glad I am no longer queen.

87

She wasn't throwing her cap in the air but, in a few months' time, she'd be able to throw her head in the air ... but not catch it.

And those bonfires would be lit under Protestants when Mary broke her promise to them.

Cruel cuts

The Duke of Northumberland was in Cambridge when he heard that Londoners had deserted him and Jane Grey. What could he do? He went into the market square with a cap full of gold coins. He threw the cap in the air, scattering the coins while he declared, 'God save Queen Mary!' While the people scrambled for the coins, his friends noticed that Northumberland was crying.

Meanwhile his servants ripped his badge off their coats and sneaked off home. They weren't going to hang around with a loser – or they might find themselves hanging around from a gallows! Northumberland was taken to the Tower of London. The mob threw mud, horse droppings (and human droppings!) at him as he was led through the streets.

Mary made another one of those treacherous Tudor promises...

I will spare the life of Lady Jane Grey.

Northumberland was the first to go. The judges passed sentence. He was guilty of treason so he was to be hanged, drawn and quartered. They added the tasty little line...

Northumberland tried every trick in the book to avoid execution. He tried weeping and pleading...

Then he tried the old Tudor trick – lying...

A couple of weeks later he climbed onto the scaffold watched by 10,000 people who hated his guts. He made a final speech in which he admitted…

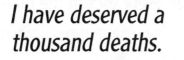 *I have deserved a thousand deaths.*

But he only got one.

Then it was Lady Jane Grey's turn. She was told she would stand trial and be found guilty, but not to worry, Queen Mary would spare her life. Fifteen-year-old Jane was pleased and said, 'She is a merciful queen!' Jane Grey had Tudor blood herself – so she should have known better!

But a Protestant rebel, Sir Thomas Wyatt, spoiled it all for her. Wyatt led a group of armed men from

Kent towards London. He said he wanted to put Lady Jane on the throne. The rebellion failed.

Mary and her ministers decided that the best way to stop any more rebellions like that was to execute Jane and her husband.

At least Jane didn't grovel like her father-in-law, Northumberland. Instead she said…

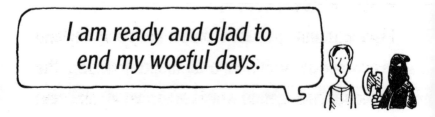

I am ready and glad to end my woeful days.

Jane acted out a scene that would have been comical if it hadn't been so gruesome. The executioner showed her the block. She knelt down and tied a handkerchief over her own eyes.

But, once she was blindfolded she couldn't remember where the block was. She waved her hands about wildly calling, 'What shall I do? Where is it?'

After an agonizing wait someone guided her hands to the block and she laid her neck on it. She died bravely. Tudor women were tough.

Foul fairs

Mary was quite popular with the people of England even though she was a Catholic. You see, the Catholics had lots of saints and every saint had their special day in the calendar, and a lot of those days were holidays. In the Middle Ages as many as one day in every three was a saint's day. How would you like that? Two days' work, one day off, two days' work, one day off.

93

The Protestants had put a stop to a lot of this saints nonsense. But there were some holidays they didn't change. The days when great fairs were held.

Forget swings, roundabouts and roller-coasters. Tudor fairs were large markets and they were dirty, dangerous and disgusting places. You'd have loved the noise, the plays and the games – but hated the cruelty to animals.

In London, the greatest fair was Saint Bartholomew's Day fair. In the Middle Ages it had been a 'cloth fair'. By Tudor times there was more fun and food and fighting than cloth! The Victorians were so disgusted by it, they finally closed it down. They would.

In Nottingham, a great goose fair started before 1540. It went on for three weeks and 20,000 geese were sold. If you've ever seen one goose's droppings then you can just about imagine the mess left by 20,000 of them!

GOOSE POO!
GOOSE POO!
GET YOUR
GOOSE POO HERE.
GREAT FOR THE
GARDEN! TWO
GROATS A BAG!

Farmers had to walk the geese to market. Sometimes they travelled for weeks. The geese were given 'shoes' of tar and sand to stop their feet from being hurt.

Not just geese were sold, but lace and cheese and willow baskets[2]. But some fairs, like Birmingham and Enfield, were mostly for selling gingerbread.

GET THOSE GEESE OFF MY GINGERBREAD!

2 A carnival is still held in Nottingham on the first weekend of October. Now it has changed to become a fun fair.

Terrible Tudor things to do on school sports day

Rope walking

At Tudor fairs a popular entertainment was to watch 'rope walkers' – men and girls who climbed on to a rope high above the ground and danced or juggled. The ropes were slack (not like a modern circus tightrope walker's) so this was a difficult trick.

Edward VI enjoyed watching one particular rope walker who attached one end of the rope to the battlements of a castle and the other end to the ground. The man then walked down to the ground without falling into the moat.

ONE'S ROPE WALKING, I THINK THE OTHER ONE'S ESCAPING

You never see that these days. What a good idea for school sports day!

Why not sponsor your head teacher to attempt it from the school roof to the field or yard below?

Flea circus

Another sad fairground loss is the flea circus. Fleas were trained to perform circus acts. They needed a trainer (to keep them up to scratch).

Flea circuses were still popular last century but have disappeared. Why are you unlikely to see this attraction at your school fete?

a They are banned by the Society Against Nastiness To Animals (SANTA).

b Fleas have become rare since the invention of the vacuum cleaner.

c Modern fleas are not as obedient as Tudor fleas and refuse to do tricks.

Answer

b The invention of the vacuum has done terrible harm to flea populations in the modern world. Cute tigers and cuddly rhinos are called 'endangered species' and are protected. Who protects the poor little flea? No one! After all the flea has done for humanity! If it wasn't for the flea we wouldn't have had the Black Death and other exciting bits of horrible history. It's about time the Society Against Flea Extermination (SAFE) jumped into action before it's too late.

PROFESSOR LIKONTI'S
wonderful Romanian
FLEA CIRCUS
Must be seen to be believed
Patronised by royalty, nobility and clergy

Come see the
LIVELY FLEAS
Dance a Ballet,
Fight a Duel with swords,
walk the tight rope,
Harnessed like
horses and drawing
and driving
wagons, mail coaches,
funeral carriages,
milk carts,
Artillery Fleas
firing a cannon.

The
Smallest Performers in the *world.*
Interesting alike to *Old* and *Young, Rich* and *Poor.*

Beware the fair

Fairs were popular places for pickpockets and cutpurses. Some criminals paid a boy to climb up a nearby church steeple. The pickpocket would cry, 'My God! Look at that!' While the crowds looked up at the boy on the steeple, the pickpocket would go through the crowd and empty their purses.

Phil death us do part

Philip II of Spain
(1527–1598)

Misery Mary's big mistake was to marry Philip of Spain in 1554. He was as popular as a piranha in a goldfish bowl. The English didn't like him because he was Spanish and he was Catholic … and Spanish Catholics were 'saving' the souls of Protestants by torturing them and burning their bodies.

102

What happened was the Church found the victims guilty and handed them over to the government. The government burned them. Philip was right – the Catholic Church didn't burn a single person. But they sent thousands to their deaths. Phil brought this charming little hobby to England.

Mary and Philip were engaged before they had even met. Mary loved her young husband madly. He was never quite so keen. As some of his unkind (but honest) courtiers said when they arrived for the wedding...

Cruellest of all was the courtier who said…

What shall the King do with such an old bitch?

What did Philip do?

I'M OFF TO FLANDERS TO FIGHT FOR SPAIN. I'LL BE BACK IN SIX WEEKS

He lied, of course. He came back over a year later for a short stay then left for good. Mary was very miserable. And every time she got miserable she decided she must have upset God. So, to make God happy, she burned more and more heretics.

A miserable Mary was a murderous Mary.

" DID YOU KNOW? MARY WAS SO DESPERATE TO GET PHILIP BACK TO ENGLAND THAT SHE ORDERED HER COOKS TO SEND HIS FAVOURITE MEAT PIES ACROSS TO FLANDERS. 'THE WAY TO A MAN'S HEART IS THROUGH HIS STOMACH,' THEY USED TO SAY. BUT THE WAY TO PHILIP'S HEART WAS NOT THROUGH MEAT PIES AND HE DIDN'T RETURN. **"**

GREAT PIES *AND* I DON'T HAVE TO LIVE WITH MARY

Hell for heretics

Mary believed that people who didn't follow the Catholic ways would roast in front of the fires of hell. These people were called 'heretics'. They had to repent (say, 'Sorry, God!') before they died. The best way to make them say 'Sorry' was to stick them on a bonfire; once they had a feel for hell-fire they would repent.

The fire would not be put out, of course. They would die whether they repented or not! But at least Mary felt sure they would go to heaven and the pain would be worthwhile.

Mary's Spanish marriage was unpopular with the English people. When the burnings started they began to really hate her.

HERETIC HOOPER'S HORROR

Today the Bishop of Gloucester, John Hooper, died horribly at the stake. He is the second victim of Queen Mary's cruel Catholic campaign. When the Queen signed his death warrant she said clearly, 'Don't try to make yourself a martyr!' But that's what he'll become after the dreadful death in Gloucester.

Hooper had a bag of gunpowder placed around his neck but it failed to explode and give him a merciful death. Instead he suffered for three-quarters of an hour, begging the spectators to fan the flames and speed the end.

One appalled spectator (who does not wish to be named) said, 'I blame the Spaniard, Philip. The sooner Mary dies and leaves the throne to Princess Elizabeth the happier we'll all be.'

The bungled execution follows the death of John Rogers in London last week. The condemned man was not even allowed to say goodbye to his wife and children. An angry crowd protested about this added cruelty. Throughout the country hundreds are being whipped in the stocks for speaking out against Queen Mary.

A woman (who does not wish to give her name) said, 'When the Queen was crowned I cheered with the rest of them. She said she'd forget that Catholic nonsense. We were cheated.'

The ashes of Hooper's fire are growing cool here in Gloucester, but the fire of anger against the Queen and her husband is burning hot and strong across the land.

Mary's cousin, Cardinal Reginald Pole, came back from Rome to help her change England back to a Catholic country. (You may remember his mum, Margaret Pole, Countess of Salisbury, who had her old head hacked off by Henry.) Reggie Pole was practically running the country for Mary.

While Mary was burning living Protestants, Reggie preferred digging up the corpses of dead heretics and burning them instead. (This does not make a lot of sense if the idea was for them to repent before they died!)

The law said that Mary had to sign every heretic's death warrant. She must have had writer's cramp because there were a lot – 240 men and 60 women. Some were popular preachers; some were simple peasants whose only crime was that they couldn't recite the Lord's Prayer.

❝DID YOU KNOW...?
A REBEL LEADER CALLED CLEOBURY WENT
AROUND EAST ANGLIA PROCLAIMING THAT MARY WAS
DEAD AND ELIZABETH SHOULD BECOME QUEEN. FEW
PEOPLE SUPPORTED HIM AND HE WAS ARRESTED.
WHEN HE WAS QUESTIONED IT TURNED OUT THAT HE
WAS A PROTESTANT AND A
CONVICTED BURGLAR. HE GAVE UP
HIS JOB TO LEAD THE
REBELLION. WHAT JOB? WHEN
HE WASN'T BURGLING HOUSES,
HE WAS A SCHOOLTEACHER! HE WAS
HANGED (FOR BEING A REBEL, NOT
FOR BEING A TEACHER).❞

Flaming Mary

Some modern historians think Mary has been treated unfairly in history books. 'She wasn't all that bad,' they say. In terms of executing people her father Henry VIII was worse. It's the horrible burnings where she's the top Tudor:

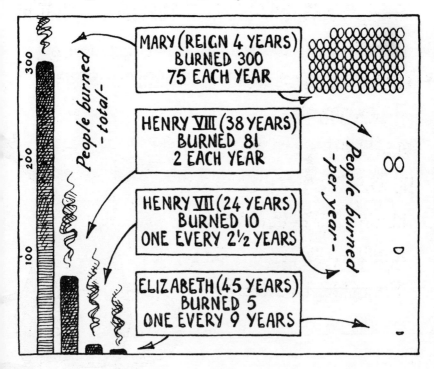

People burned - total -

People burned - per year -

MARY (REIGN 4 YEARS)
BURNED 300
75 EACH YEAR

HENRY VIII (38 YEARS)
BURNED 81
2 EACH YEAR

HENRY VII (24 YEARS)
BURNED 10
ONE EVERY 2½ YEARS

ELIZABETH (45 YEARS)
BURNED 5
ONE EVERY 9 YEARS

Truesome but gruesome

As Mary lay dying, England and France were at war. Philip's Spain was at war with France so wife Mary's England had to join in ... whether they liked it or not! A peace treaty was brought to Mary for her to sign but she was too ill with influenza to read it. The documents stayed by her bedside. When she died the next day her ministers looked for the papers by the bedside ... but they had vanished.

After searching the room from top to bottom they questioned Mary's chief lady-in-waiting. 'Have you seen any long rolls of parchment?'

'Long rolls of parchment? Oh, yes. They were so useful I used them all up.'

'Used them for what?'

'Why, to wrap up the Queen's corpse!'

Disgusting diseases

If you catch influenza (flu) you'll probably get a couple of days off school. If you are really ill (or a good actor) you may get a week off school. But Tudor flu would make sure you never went back to school again – it could kill you as it killed Queen Mary I.

The Tudors didn't understand about germs. They thought sickness was carried in bad smells – in which case your dad's socks would be a deadly weapon! So it's not surprising there were a lot of terrible Tudor dangers to overcome if you wanted to reach old age … or even school age. Try this quick quiz to see how much more you understand about illness and disease than your Tudor ancestors…

True or false?

a The thing that killed most sailors was shipwrecks.

b Elizabeth I had the disease smallpox and survived.

c Only prisoners caught 'jail fever'.

d Henry VII's coronation was delayed because he had 'sweating sickness'.

e Some Elizabethans believed that going to the theatre was the cause of the plague.

Answers

a False. The disease 'scurvy' killed more sailors than shipwrecks, wars at sea and all other diseases put together. When they went on long voyages they

hadn't enough fresh fruit and vegetables so they didn't get enough vitamin C. The result was disgusting and you wouldn't want to know … but here it is anyway. After three months you'd feel tired and have no energy. After five months your skin becomes rough and dry. By six months your legs start to bleed and if you get a wound it won't heal. From seven to eight months your gums go soft, swell up and turn purple. The teeth become loose and old wounds begin to open up. If you've had no fresh fruit or veg by nine months you'll have heart and lung problems that can kill you … but you'll feel so rotten that death would make a nice change!

ACHE ACHE

b **True**. Elizabeth caught smallpox at the age of 29. This charming disease gives you a high temperature and pains in the head and the muscles. This sometimes ended with the lungs filling with blood and the patient dying. But, if you survived another two to five days, then a rash appeared that grew into great pimples. These burst and the scabs dropped off after a few weeks, but the scars they left behind were with you for life. This was one reason why Elizabeth wore thick white make-up. Her devoted lady-in-waiting, Lady Sydney, caught the disease from nursing the Queen. Lady Sydney survived but her face was so damaged that she left the royal court and hid herself away for the rest of her life. (Why didn't she just stay and wear a paper bag over her head?)

c False. 'Jail fever' was a form of the Typhus disease. It arrived in England in 1522 during the reign of Henry VIII. The first outbreak was in  Cambridge where it spread from the prisoners to everyone in the courtroom. The jury, the spectators and the judges all caught the fever which also gave them a red rash over their bodies. More than half of the victims survived but no one understood what caused this dread disease. In fact, it is carried by lice – head lice (nits) and body lice. People in crowded, dirty conditions like ships, armies and jails shared their lice and the lice carried the germs from one to another. The really, really, sad thing is that the poor innocent little lice caught the disease too and they died! They didn't ask to be locked up in a jail with all those filthy humans! (Can't you just picture a tragic louse with a high temperature and a rash? How did it feel? Lousy!)

d False. It was delayed because many people in London had this plague. 'Sweating sickness' was a Tudor disease which arrived with Henry Tudor at

TINKLE TINKLE

the Battle of Bosworth Field. It's probable that the disease was carried by the soldiers he brought with him from France. Sweating sickness (or 'the sweat') arrived without warning in the morning or at night. Shivering was followed by sweating and then terrible weakness. If your body stopped sweating then you started peeing. If you survived two days then you'd probably live. Many died in the first 24 hours. The good news is that children and wrinklies were spared this disease usually, and so were the poor. It struck more upper-class men and, weirdly, seemed to stop at the Borders of Scotland every time it broke out. Maybe the disease hated the bagpipes!

e True. In the 1590s the plague spread though Tudor England repeatedly – usually in the summer. London magistrates closed the theatre to stop it spreading. But

some religious people believed the theatre caused the plague. They said the theatre was wicked and God punished theatre-goers by giving them the plague. What would they have said about television?

1558

Mary's half-sister **Elizabeth takes the throne** and, typical Tudor, changes everything around. She tells the English that they are going to be Protestants again.

1587

Queen Bess's cousin, Catholic Mary, Queen of Scots, is a menace. She's been thrown out of Scotland and imprisoned in England ... but is plotting to break free and murder Bess. The English Queen remembers her father's fast fix for wicked women and has **Mary's head lopped off**.

1588

Phil's back. The Catholic king of Spain wants his dead wife's throne. He tries to invade with an armada of ships but English navy nobbles him.

1603

Queen Bess, the last Tudor, dies. James, son of Mary, Queen of Scots, comes down from Edinburgh to rule. Terrible Tudors terminated. **Slimy Stuarts succeed**.

Queen Elizabeth I
(reigned 1558–1603)

Queen Elizabeth had her father's bad temper and her grandfather's meanness. Both Elizabeth and her big sister Mary enjoyed playing cards. Mary was a loser, but Elizabeth won a fortune. Why?

Was it because Elizabeth was a skilful player?

No. It was because no one dared to beat her! If she lost, she sulked or lost her temper. It was easier (but expensive) to let Elizabeth win. While most Tudor workers were lucky to earn two or three pounds a year from working, one of Elizabeth's courtiers, Lord North, lost ten pounds every week at playing cards with the Queen[3] He was almost ruined. Here's an Elizabethan card game you may like to try. You can play it against friends – for matchsticks, not for money!

[3] Lord North was the Treasurer. His job was to look after England's money. If the Tudors knew the way he lost so much at cards they'd have been very worried! Would you trust that man with your money?

Mumchance at cards

You need:

- A pack of playing cards.
- Two or more players.

To play:

The cards are shuffled and placed face down on a table.

Each player in turn calls the name of a card – everyone has to name a different card. The cards are turned over one at a time. The player whose card is turned over first wins a point.

The first to ten points is the winner.

Advanced play: Do not shuffle the cards each time. Instead place the turned cards to one side. Good players will remember which cards have been turned over and will not name them.

Crafty card sharps

It wasn't only the Queen who took money off people at cards. There were criminals called 'cozeners' who made money out of victims they called 'conies'.

This is how they did it…

Coney catching for a profit

London is full of them! Conies from the countryside with fat purses just waiting to be emptied. Here's how to do it.

You need:

- A gold coin.
- A few silver shillings.
- A partner (your 'barnacle').
- A pack of marked cards or a pair of trick dice.

1 First catch your coney. Go to St Paul's Churchyard where all the farm fools gather. Listen for one who speaks with a curious accent. If they say, 'Oooh! Arrrrh!' then you know that he's a coney. Now, drop the gold coin on the ground so that he can't miss it. As he bends to pick it up say, 'Ah! You saw it at the same moment as me. I'll tell you what – let's share it.' With any luck he'll say, 'Oooh! Arrrrh!' then tell him you need to go to a local tavern to change it and offer to buy a drink with your half.

2 Show him a card game and bet a shilling or two. Make sure that he wins about five shillings from you. Then say, 'You're so good you should be playing someone with much more money.' Then point to your barnacle and say, 'That man over there is rich – and stupid. Let's invite him to have a game.' With any luck he'll say, 'Oooh! Arrrrh!'

3 Let the coney win a pile of money from your barnacle. Then raise the stakes till he is betting with all the money in his purse. When all of his money is on the table then make sure he loses. Your barnacle takes the pot of money and shares it with you later. Say, 'Bad luck,' to the coney. He'll probably say, 'Oooh! Arrrrh!'

Other tricks included selling tickets for plays – plays that were never performed! A man called Richard Vennor tried this and pocketed all of the money. But, in the end, he was caught and thrown in prison.

At first, Vennor used his money to buy a private cell, good food and wine from the jailer. But, when the money ran out, he was thrown in 'The Hole' with 50 other men to sleep on bare boards with 50 other men, women and children. The cold in winter or the disease in summer or the bad food killed anyone who stayed too long. The poet, Thomas Dekker, said that in The Hole you are 'buried before you are dead'. Richard Vennor died.

Cozening can be bad for your health!

Potty plots

The first Tudor, Henry VII, had many plots against his life to deal with. His granddaughter, Elizabeth I, was no different. Some of the plots were serious and some were just hoaxes. The Essex rebellion in 1601 was real enough though.

Elizabeth had a favourite young courtier, the Earl of Essex. But the trouble started back in 1594, when Elizabeth became annoyed with him. He had to do something to win back her friendship. He came up with the idea of rescuing Elizabeth from a plot against her life.

So Essex wrote to the Queen…

Your Gracious Majesty,
*   I write with sad and*
worrying news. My spies (who
work for your protection even though
they cost me a lot of my own money)
have uncovered a plot. It seems they
have heard that your doctor,
Roderigo Lopez, has been paid by
his Spanish masters to poison you.
Lopez, as you know, is Jewish. Jews
are not popular and you would be
most popular if you had him executed.
If I have saved your life with this
news then I am well rewarded.
*   Your most humble servant*

*   Essex*

The Queen took the letter seriously. She then called her own ministers to question all the Spanish spies they could find and uncover the truth.

She was furious … with Essex.

My Lord Essex,
     I have looked into your claims against Doctor Lopez most carefully. It seems the man is innocent. Your spies are fools… and so is their master. Do not bother me with this matter again.
                    ELizabeth

Essex's plan had gone badly wrong. What could he do?

And that's just what Essex did for two days. Then he had another idea…

Essex had all the people Lopez worked with brought to his dungeons…

But, when the witnesses were faced with torture, they changed their story … wouldn't you?

Elizabeth had to believe in the doctor's guilt now. The poor man was sent to the scaffold where he died a traitor's death.

But oh yes, he almost certainly was.

Sadly, Lopez and the witnesses weren't the only victims of the Earl's cruel plot. The English people turned against all the Jews in England, beat them, robbed them and drove them from their homes.

Even the playwright William Shakespeare cashed in on the hatred of Jews by writing a play with a Jewish villain, *The Merchant of Venice*. It was a huge success ... except with the suffering Jews, of course.

Essex's end

Not every plot against Elizabeth was so harmless. But the most dangerous one was led by Essex, the man who sent Doctor Lopez to his dreadful death. It served him right that his plot failed and he was executed. He was lucky that he didn't suffer the way Lopez had.

The problem was that the Queen was getting old and feeble. Essex reckoned it was time she handed over the real power to someone young and fit. Someone just like him, in fact.

The rebellion caused a sensation at the time. If there had been newspapers in Elizabeth's day, then the front pages may have looked something like this…

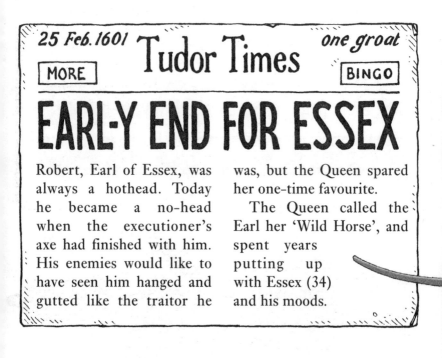

25 Feb. 1601 **Tudor Times** one groat

MORE   BINGO

EARL-Y END FOR ESSEX

Robert, Earl of Essex, was always a hothead. Today he became a no-head when the executioner's axe had finished with him. His enemies would like to have seen him hanged and gutted like the traitor he was, but the Queen spared her one-time favourite.

The Queen called the Earl her 'Wild Horse', and spent years putting up with Essex (34) and his moods.

He could be charming when he wanted and the handsome young tearaway knew how to flatter the old Queen.

The Earl thought the people of England were ready for a new leader. There have been years of famine in which poor people have died on the streets or fed their children on cats, dogs and nettle roots.

Essex decided he was the man to lead them into a new century and a new age. He rode at the head of 100 horsemen into the city of London. But the 'most popular man in England' (as he has been called) found that no one would join him.

He was arrested and the Queen's only mercy was to let him be beheaded. Today is a sad day for Her Majesty. Her people still support her but the last of her young favourites is dead. She'll be lonely now with nothing to look forward to but death.

Liz's loo

Queen Elizabeth travelled around the south of England and stayed in the houses of gentlemen and ladies. If you ever got a letter from the Queen saying, 'I am coming to stay with you!' then you might have been thrilled.

You might also have been horrified. The Queen's careless courtiers could easily leave your home a wreck.

Queen Liz expected...

- your best rooms for herself and her lords (while you moved out and lived in an inn or a tent).
- rich gifts – gold and jewels were best.
- entertainments – music, plays and sports.

The honour was great … but the cost could be greater. It wasn't just the homes of gentlemen that had to fork out. It was the ordinary people of the places she visited.

A grammar school in Norwich paid out nine shillings and four pence (two weeks' wages for a teacher) just to paint the door and clean up three loads of 'street muck' outside. The nervous headmaster gave a speech (in Latin) and she let him kiss her hand. What a treat for Liz – would you like to have your hand kissed by a head teacher?

Everywhere Elizabeth went, her people spent a fortune cleaning the place up. She must have thought England was a really tidy place!

On that visit to Norwich the people of the city were given orders weeks before she arrived…

- Put fresh plaster on the fronts of your houses (just the side the queen would see)
- Clean up your outside toilets
- Repair the path outside your house
- Keep your cows off the streets - milk them in the fields or your yard
- Sweep your chimneys (fine for a chimney fire - 6 shillings and 8 pence)

In addition, butchers who killed cattle inside the city had to take the waste outside and bury it. Makes you wonder what they did with it before. No cows, pigs or horses were to be kept in the castle ditch.

Why did Elizabeth make her people go to all this trouble? There were two good reasons ... and one other that most history books don't mention...

1 Elizabeth wanted her people to see her – she loved being cheered by her faithful subjects.

2 The plague came to London most summers and it was safer to travel round in the fresher air of the countryside.[4]

3 Toilets.

4 But the court often brought the plague with it and hundreds of townspeople died after Elizabeth left. After the Queen left Norwich, 5,000 people died of plague. Some of her hosts were dead honoured after her visit – others were simply dead.

Toilets? (You are probably asking yourself!) What have toilets got to do with the Queen going on a tour about the countryside. (Even if you are not asking yourself this, you are going to be told.)

In Tudor England the great houses and palaces had little rooms just like in your house. The Tudor name was 'jakes'. But the waste from the jakes didn't get washed away. It fell down into a pit. With hundreds of people living in a palace these pits soon filled up … and up … and up.

The pits had to be opened up, the waste shovelled up and carted away. (There's a nice job for someone … preferably someone without a sense of smell.)

While this was going on it was pretty disgusting in your palace. The smell would hang around for weeks. The best thing to do would be to fill up your jakes, then move out while they were emptied. That's what the Tudor monarchs did. That's why they had three or four palaces and kept moving around. Best of all, Elizabeth could move around to other people's houses and fill up their jakes! Then she could move on and leave some other poor person (or poo person) to clear up after her.

What is the greatest gift you could give your queen? A pair of golden spurs? A pair of jewelled gloves? A pair of solid silver nose-hair clippers?

No. It would be a flushing toilet. And that's just what her godson, Sir John Harrington did…

21 May 1589

Your most Illustrious and beautiful majesty,

It is almost six years now since you banished me from court. I deserved it. The joke I made about Kate Sedley's chest was extremely rude and I quite understand why she was so upset. I also understand why you told me to leave your palace and never return.

But you are my Godmother and such a sweet, kindly person, I thought perhaps you may have forgiven me enough to come and visit me. Let me tell you what I have been doing in the six years that I have been away.

Of course I was heart-broken at your displeasure. A day without seeing you is like a day without sunshine. I came home to my old family estate in Somerset and wept for weeks. Then I decided on my great project. I decided to build a new house,

145

a great house, and a house with an invention so magical you would have to come and visit me.

You see, when I built Kelston Hall I built in a special toilet system. It works with water. The person entering the jakes sits on a comfortable wooden seat. When they have finished then they pull a lever and water from a tank above the toilet rushes down. The foul-smelling waste is washed away down drains to a deep pit. The result is the sweetest smelling house you ever imagined.

If you will excuse my little joke. I call my invention "Ajax" after the Greek hero – and because I invented "a jakes" Ha! You always did like my jokes, dear Godmother. But please, please come to Kelston Hall. Please forgive me and please inspect Ajax.

Your loving Godson

John

Suppose you were Queen Elizabeth. What would you do if you got a letter saying, 'I'm sorry about my rude joke six years ago but, if you forgive me, you could come and see my new toilet'?

What did Elizabeth do?
a Ignore the letter.
b Visit John and forgive him.
c Have him drowned in his own toilet bowl.

Answer

b The Queen was in a forgiving mood. She went across to Kelston Hall in the summer of 1591 and used the Ajax. She was delighted with it! Not only did she forgive her godson, but she invited him back to London to fit his toilet invention in all of her palaces.

Elizabeth was the first monarch in Britain to have a flushing toilet. It was healthier – and far less smelly – than the old jakes, yet it was another 200 years before the idea really caught on and was used in a lot of houses.

Quick quiz

What did the Elizabethans use instead of toilet paper?

Answer

A damp rag. It could be rinsed and used over again. (Oh, stop pulling a disgusted face. It was probably better than the hard toilet paper your mum and dad used to use!) In really nasty prisons you weren't even given a cloth. And you thought school detention was bad?

Would you believe it?

Here are some curious tales about the days of Queen Liz. But which are true and which are false? Pester your parent and blow their brain cell with this quick quiz.

1 Queen Elizabeth ate a chessboard.

2 In her last years Elizabeth carried a rusty old sword around her palace in case she was attacked.

3 Elizabeth stayed alive with the help of expensive medicines.

4 John Stubbs wrote and criticized Elizabeth's plan to marry a Frenchman, so Elizabeth had Stubbs's hand cut off.

5 When the Spanish Armada sailed to England, Elizabeth was brave and ready to face them.

6 When sister Mary Tudor was queen, Elizabeth wore finer dresses than Mary.

7 Elizabeth invented the nickname 'Bloody Mary' for her sister.

8 When Queen Mary died she left a will. Elizabeth ignored it.

9 Elizabeth's pet name for Sir Walter Raleigh was 'Water'.

10 Elizabeth kept her breath fresh with mint mouthwash.

Answers

1 True. It was made from her favourite food – marzipan – shaped into black and white squares. In fact she ate so much of this sticky sweet that it rotted her teeth till they were as black and white as the chessboard ... mate!

2 True. She was terrified of being assassinated. A sailor and a gang of men burst into the room where she was eating with her ladies-in-waiting. He had already drawn his dagger to strike before the guards managed to stop him. Elizabeth banned her courtiers from wearing long cloaks because she wanted their swords uncovered and ready – she even threatened to pass a law against long cloaks! (And Little Red Riding Hood would have had to change her name to Little Red Bomber Jacket!)

3 False. Elizabeth hated taking medicine. She kept fit with lots of walking and riding. The doctors said all the exercise would kill her but in fact in the last six years of her reign she had five different doctors …

and they all died before her! In the end she went for walkies in the rain, caught a cold and never recovered. If the Queen had had a pair of wellies she might have lived even longer.

4 True. Elizabeth considered marrying Francis, Duke of Anjou but many English people were horrified because he was a Catholic. Stubbs was brave enough (or stupid enough) to write a leaflet attacking her. The punishment was to cut off the hand that wrote it. Stubbs used his remaining hand to wave his hat in

the air and cry, 'God save the Queen!' …
before he fainted. The publisher also had his
hand cut off – a sharp lesson to all publishers
who write nasty things about the royal family!

THOSE WERE THE DAYS

5 False (probably). She is famous for her
speech to the troops as they waited for the
Spanish to land: 'I have the body of a weak and
feeble woman, but I have the heart and stomach
of a king.' Modern historians are not sure if she
really made the speech … but, even if she did,

not many would have heard it. As for her courage, a lot of her soldiers said she had none.

CAN'T I MAKE THE SPEECH FROM HERE?

6 False. Elizabeth was crafty. Her supporters were the Protestants who hated flashy clothes. Elizabeth wore black and white to please them. Mary was angry and wanted Elizabeth to dress in rich materials with jewels. Once Mary died and Elizabeth became queen, then she gave up the plain clothes and wore dresses encrusted with jewels. The dresses could stand up by themselves!

7 False. Mary I is usually known as Bloody Mary but no one in Tudor times called her that. They probably wouldn't dare! The name was invented about a hundred years after her death. In Mary's own time she was called 'a raging madwoman' and 'mischievous Mary'.

8 True. Elizabeth didn't become a Catholic as Mary had asked, she didn't bury Catherine of Aragon beside her daughter Mary and she certainly didn't give King Philip of Spain his jewels back!

RIPPERTY RIP!

9 True. But it wasn't because he was wet. Sir Walter came from Devon and spoke with a strong Devon accent. When he said, 'My name is Walter,' it sounded like, 'My name is Water.' Water funny thing to say!

10 False. Elizabeth used a mixture with lots of sugar in it. Of course, this rotted her teeth. Good dentists said Tudor people should use wooden toothpicks and they were right. But rich people used gold or silver ones that damaged their teeth. So, if you want to suffer like Liz then rinse your mouth out with lemonade three times a day and the tooth fairy will be a regular visitor to your house!

Devilish Doctor Dee
John Dee (1527–1608)

John Dee was a maths teacher who had some daft ideas about making gold from cheap metal. But he did come up with one good idea that made Elizabeth a fortune. One of his maths skills was in map-making. It is probable that he showed the Queen how it would be possible for English ships to reach South America and return safely.

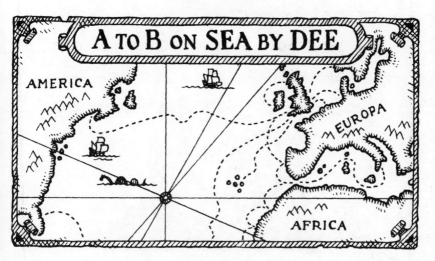

All the Queen needed was a skilful sailor who could follow Dee's charts and be bold enough to attack every Spanish port and Spanish ship he found there. There was one man who was just right for the job – a brilliant sailor and a ruthless pirate – Francis Drake.

Drake the quacker

Sir Francis Drake (around 1542–1596)

When it came to making money, Queen Elizabeth was ruthless. She looked greedily at the Spanish treasure ships and decided she wanted her share.

The Spanish didn't like Elizabeth and her England too much. After all, the Spanish king, Philip, had been married to her sister, Mary…

I SHOULD HAVE TAKEN THE ENGLISH THRONE WHEN MARY DIED

R.I.P.

And, of course, Elizabeth was a protestant…

NOT ONLY THAT! SHE IS HELPING OTHER PROTESTANTS REBEL AGAINST SPANISH RULE

YA!

YA BOO!

161

So, the Spanish didn't like the English. They weren't going to give Queen Liz their silver...

I'LL JUST HAVE TO ARRANGE TO HAVE THE STUFF PINCHED. CAPTAIN FRANCIS DRAKE IS THE MAN TO DO IT

Elizabeth told Drake she would 'gladly be revenged on the King of Spain' ... but the money was as important as the revenge.

Francis's fun

Francis Drake was not usually seen as a cruel man – even by his deadly Spanish enemies. But one trick was a bit vicious.

Drake's men captured a Spanish ship in a South American harbour. Most of the crew had jumped overboard and swam ashore, but Drake captured one young sailor alive. There was no treasure loaded on to the ship. It must be somewhere on shore. Drake didn't want to waste time looking for it.

He turned to his captive. 'Tell me where I'll find the silver when I get ashore.'

'I'll tell you nothing,' the brave young Spaniard said.

'Tell me or I'll hang you.'

'You are not a murderer, Captain Drake. You won't hang me.'

'Won't I?' Drake laughed. He ordered a rope to be thrown over one of the ship's spars. He tied the sailor's hands and stood him on the edge of the ship. Then he placed the rope around his neck. 'Now will you tell me?'

The Spaniard trembled, shook his head and said, 'You wouldn't.'

'Wouldn't I?' Drake placed a hand against the young man's knee and pushed him till he tumbled off the side of the ship.

The sailor screamed as he fell and the scream stopped only when the sailor hit the water. The rope around his neck had not been fastened to anything and it didn't choke the prisoner. Drake told him to hold on to the rope and hauled him back on the ship. By now the man was so terrified he told Drake everything he wanted to know.

That's cruel.

Francis's failure

In 1580 Francis Drake was knighted by the Queen for his efforts. He was her favourite feller. Of course the Queen said, 'Let's do it again!'

In 1585 she paid half of the £40,000 costs to send Drake back to South America. Of course, the Spanish were ready for him this time and he was beaten again and again. He returned with just £30,000 in treasure – the Queen lost £5,000 and Drake lost 750 men, including some of his best captains.

Queen Elizabeth was Misery Liz. Drake wasn't her pet any longer.

But Spain's king was Furious Phil. He sent the great Armada, a fleet of 130 ships, against England in 1588 and Drake helped to defeat it. Drake was back in favour.

The Queen decided to follow the Spanish back to their home and destroy their ships before they could send another armada against England. In 1589 Drake was put in charge of the attack on Spain ... and failed. No treasure and over 10,000 men dead this time! Misery Liz again!

So Drake offered to go on one more voyage to the Americas to steal Spanish treasure in 1595. He was sick and old now and it wasn't a Spanish cannon that finished him off. It was much sadder.

Many poems have been written about Drake, the great hero. A lot of the poems were written by his old enemies, the Spanish.

In one poem, he is poisoned by his English sailors because he failed on his last expedition. This spiteful Spanish verse ended…

'I come, I come; oh fearful Death, I come!'
With that Drake died, his frozen
tongue was still.
The staring pupils flickered now no more;
The purple mouth, cold with the chill of death,
Spat out his wicked soul; out from his breast
Into the deep and endless mouth of Hell.

Cheerful stuff, but nonsense. Here is the horrible historical truth...

Dead duck Drake

Drake was in the Indies and he wasn't doing well.

His men were falling sick, and dropping dead.

The Spanish sailors fought real hard,

and gave the English hell.

'Ohhhh! I don't feel too grand,' Sir Francis said.

He lay down in his cabin and the fever

made him sick.

The doctor said, 'You'll die before you're older!'

Then Drake he made his will and he said,

'Bring my armour quick!

If I'm to die then I'll die like a soldier!'

He fastened on his armour then he lay down
on his bed,
His sailors gathered round to say goodbye.
Within an hour the brave old Francis Drake
was lying dead,
And tears ran down from every sailor's eye.

They wrapped his poor old body in a coffin
made of lead,
So fishes couldn't eat him and get fat.
They dropped the coffin in the sea.
'Goodbye old Drake,' they said.
They sailed back home again …
and that was that!

Mary, Queen of chops

Mary, Queen of Scots:
Queen in Scotland
(reigned 1542–1568)
Died 1587

Mary, Queen of Scots became queen of Scotland when she was just six days old. (She probably celebrated by wetting her nappy.) Her great grandfather was Henry VII, so she was a Tudor. That meant she enjoyed plotting and murdering her enemies, not to mention her friends and relatives. Being a Tudor, she got away with it – until she came up against another Tudor, that is!

Mary was forced to leave Scotland when she got into a bit of trouble for having her husband murdered. (He deserved it.) She fled to England and asked for cousin Elizabeth's protection. Elizabeth I had Mary arrested and locked away for 19 years. But there were always Catholics plotting to kill Elizabeth and put Mary on the throne of England. Mary had to go.

Elizabeth always said she didn't want the blame for killing cousin Mary, but...

• Elizabeth's spies trapped Mary into saying she wanted Elizabeth dead, then...

• After a trial, Elizabeth signed Mary's death warrant, though...

• Elizabeth sent a message to Mary's jailer suggesting it would be better if Mary was quietly murdered!

When the jailer refused to murder Mary then the execution had to go ahead. These are the foul facts...

Foul facts about Mary's execution

Mary didn't know she was going to die till the night before it happened. She stayed awake all night, writing letters and praying. It would have been difficult to sleep, anyway, with guards marching up and down outside her room and the scaffold being hammered together in the great hall. By the time she got to the block she must have been ready to nod off!

I DON'T SUPPOSE I COULD HAVE A PILLOW?

Mary's jailers refused to let her have a Catholic priest to pray with her. This was a bit spiteful.

They gave her a Protestant who was still trying to convert her when she was on the scaffold! She simply said, 'I've lived a Catholic, so I will die a Catholic.' This didn't stop him going on and on. Mary's servants read a Bible story with her. It was the story of the good thief who died on the cross alongside Jesus. Mary heard it and said, 'That thief was a great sinner – but not such a great sinner as I have been.' Maybe she was thinking of the husband she had murdered.

The Scottish Queen was not allowed to die quietly. Three hundred people crowded into the hall to watch her execution. The scaffold was decorated in a delightful shade of black and it made a very pleasant day out for the spectators. Some reported that she came into the hall 'cheerful and smiling', so that was all right.

OOOH, NICE TURN-OUT THEN

Mary was dressed in black until the time came for her to die. She took her dress off and was wearing a red petticoat. She slipped on red sleeves and was all in red, so the blood wouldn't show. That's tidy, isn't it? She wore a turban round her head to keep her hair out of the way of the axe. Her eyes were bound with a white cloth, trimmed in gold.

The axe-man's assistant held her body steady while the axe fell. It missed the neck and cut into the back of her head. Her servants later said they heard her mutter, 'Sweet Jesus.' The second chop was a better shot but it still needed a bit of sawing with the axe to finish it off.

Mary's pet dog, a skye terrier, had slipped into the hall under the cover of her skirts and was still hiding there when her head was lopped off. It finally came out, whimpering. It's said that the dog refused to eat and pined away and died. Mary's heart was removed – the English didn't want any of that Robert the Bruce nonsense with loyal Scots following a heart into battle. The heart was buried in the castle grounds and hasn't been seen since. Mary asked to be buried in France. So, of course, she was buried in Peterborough, which is not the same thing at all. In 1612, her son, by then James I of England, had her coffin moved to Westminster Abbey where it is today.

Meanwhile, at Fotheringhay, the Scottish national flower, the thistle, was growing. People said they sprang from the tears of Mary, Queen of Scots.

THISTLE BE WHERE SHE DIED

CLICK

Gloriana the gory

The Elizabethan age is famous for its theatre. Great writers like Shakespeare and Marlowe began to create plays which are performed all around the world to this day. One of the greatest fans was the Queen herself (nicknamed Gloriana).

But where did these great plays come from? Did William Shakespeare just sit down one day and say...

I AM GOING TO WRITE A GREAT PLAY!

Of course not. In the Middle Ages, the workers in the towns had produced religious plays, often based on Bible stories. But they weren't just a way of preaching to people on stage. They were FUN...

Devils sprang from trapdoors.
God and his angels swooped
down from cranes.
Hell's mouth opened and
belched out smoke.
Floods, fires and earthquakes
were staged.
Characters suffered gory
executions and wounds.
Animals like rabbits and rams
appeared as sacrifices.
Costumes and masks were
dazzling.
Singing and dancing was loud
and lively.

BOING!

SWING

SHAKE!

BANG
BANG

Henry VIII's chopping and changing of the Church changed all that.

What a loss! Imagine if today's Queen pulled the plug on all your television! People would miss it.

Poets started writing plays for students to perform in their colleges. A teacher, Nicholas Udal, wrote a play for his pupils to perform in front of Elizabeth.

But what could the ordinary people do for fun?

SHLOP!

WOW! HOW DO YOU DO THAT!

There were street entertainers doing disgusting things for money. One man pretended to stab himself in the stomach. In fact, he had a bag of pig's blood under his shirt and a wooden shield under that. When he was stabbed, the pig's blood spurted out and the audience gasped with wonder (or threw up in horror). One drunken entertainer forgot the shield one day, stabbed himself in the stomach and died. The audience thought that was the best trick they'd ever seen!

A juggler called Kingsfield showed the body of 'John the Baptist' who'd had his head cut off – the head lay at the feet and it spoke!

Then there was always the torturing of animals for sport. In the courtyards of inns and special buildings there was cock-fighting, bear-baiting and bull-baiting. In 1584 a foreign visitor to the Beargarden in London described the cheerful little scene...

There is a round building three stories high in which are kept about a hundred large English dogs, with separate wooden kennels for each of them. These dogs were made to fight one at a time with three bears, the second bear being larger than the first and the third larger than the second. After this a horse was brought in and chased by the dogs and, at the end, a bull who defended himself bravely.

WHO LET THE CAT OUT?

The trouble is the bears needed a rest every other day. What could the bear-pit owners do to entertain the Elizabethans on the bear's day off? Put on the plays!

Don't give them the clever poetic plays of the students. Give them a bit of the old glamour and guts of the old religious plays.

But don't give them the religion of those old plays, of course – religion could get you hanged, burned and chopped in Tudor times!

Instead they went back to the Roman theatre. They took ideas from writers like Seneca. His favourite subjects were crime and revenge, witches and ghosts, and they were very popular. The Romans loved tales of horror. Shakespeare probably read Seneca's gruesome plays at school.

William Shakespeare was a clever man. When he started writing at the end of the 1580s he was going to give the Beargarden mob the sort of fun they wanted … he was going to give them horror.

If the plays of the Elizabethan playwrights Marlowe, Kyd and Shakespeare were produced today they would be given an 18 certificate.

Terrible Titus

Titus Andronicus was probably one of Shakespeare's earliest plays. You won't see it performed much these days. Here's this charming tale of family fun … and fingernails.

Perform this potted play for school governors, parents and teachers. But have the sick-bags handy.

Cast:

Titus Andronicus – old Roman general, losing his marbles.

Lucius – Titus's last-remaining son.

Tamora – Queen of the defeated Goths, prisoner of Titus and a nasty piece of work.

Alarbus – eldest son of Tamora and quite inflammable.

Chiron and Demetrius – Tamora's younger sons. Suckers.

Aaron – Tamora's boyfriend. A bit of a stirrer and a lot of a murderer.

Bassianus and Saturninus – Sons of the dead Roman emperor. Not very brotherly.

Lavinia – Titus's daughter. Engaged to Saturninus till Bassianus snatches her and she is really cut up about it.

Servants can be played by those who die early on in the play.

Scene 1 – Titus's palace in Rome.

(Titus and Tamora meet)

Titus: Oh dear! Oh dear! Oh dear! Twenty-five sons I had at one time! Twenty-five! And how many have I got now? Four! After that battle with your Goths! Four! It's all your fault, Tamora. I'm going to have your oldest lad executed.

Tamora: You can't do that, you swine! That's not fair!

Titus: Bassianus and Saturninus! Fetch Tamora's son. (Enter Bassianus and Saturninus with Alarbus) Yes, General.

Titus: Take Tamora's son, Alarbus. Take him to the altar, cut him into pieces then burn him as a sacrifice to my dead sons.

Alarbus: That's not very fair, Mum!

Tamora: I told him that, son, but the old fool won't listen.

Alarbus: (Led off by Bassianus) Bye, Mum.

Tamora: Bye, son.

Titus: As for you, Saturninus ... I do not want the job of emperor. I hereby elect you!

Saturninus: Thanks, boss!

Titus: And you can marry my daughter, Lavinia.

Saturninus: Even better. This is my lucky day!

Alarbus: (Voice from off-stage) I wish it was mine! Ouch!

(They all leave the stage. Enter Lucius.)

Lucius: (Narrating) Before Lavinia could marry Saturninus, she saw Tamora's boyfriend, Aaron, kill Bassianus. To silence her Aaron cut out her tongue. To stop her writing the name of the killer he cut off her hands. Titus saw one of his sons killed by Bassianus and another two murdered by Saturninus — even though Titus had cut off his own hand in an attempt to get mercy for them. That left me, Lucius, as his last son and handless Lavinia as his last daughter.

Titus: So who did this to you, Lavinia? Here ... take this stick and write it in the sand ... (He reads) Tamora! Fetch her sons, Chiron and Demetrius to me, Lavinia ... and fetch a big bowl. (Lavinia enters with Chiron and Demetrius)

Chiron: What can I do for you, old chap?

Titus: Kneel down, boys. Now, Lavinia, hold that bowl to catch the blood while I cut their throats. (Chiron and Demetrius try to run. Titus catches them off-stage. Lavinia hurries after with the bowl.)

Scene 2 – The palace a few days later.

(Enter Tamora and Saturninus, Titus, Lavinia and Lucius)

Titus: Have this nice pie I had specially baked.

Tamora: (Helping herself) Yummy! But hang on – yeuch! This is a human fingernail!

Titus: That's right. You have ruined my daughter's life. There's nothing left for her but death. So, here it is! (He stabs Lavinia)

Tamora: Never mind her! What was in that pie?

Titus: Your last two sons … Chiron and Demetrius. You've just eaten them!

Tamora: Yeuuuurrrrggggh!

Titus: Now it's your turn, Queen terrible Tamora! (He stabs Tamora)

Saturninus: Now it's your turn, old twithead Titus! (He stabs Titus)

Lucius: Now it's your turn, savage Saturninus! (He stabs Saturninus then calls…) Servants! Feed Tamora to the wild beasts and bury the rest. (To audience) I guess that makes me emperor since I'm the last one left alive! The end!

THE END!

That was Elizabeth's entertainment. Murders, executions and sacrifices – heads and hands cut off, on stage. Sons served up in a pie to their mother.

Queen Elizabeth loved it – and so would you, probably. But would your parents let you watch it?

Compared to the real-life, bloodthirsty executions, of course, the blood on the stage was just harmless fun!

In *Titus Andronicus*, Shakespeare was trying to grab the attention of his horror-loving audience. But he was still putting plenty of gore and shocks into his plays ten or 20 years later. Shakespeare shockers included…

- a character having his eyes ripped out on stage (*King Lear*)

- a king beheaded in a sword fight (*Macbeth*)

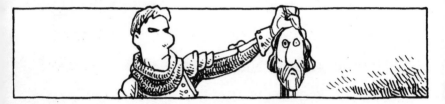

- a real bear chasing a character off the stage (*The Winter's Tale*).

TEST YOUR TUDOR TEACHER...

Teachers don't know everything. Amazing but true! But they test you and expect you to know it. So it's only fair they should face a sort of Tudor torture. (Or the threat of double helpings of school dinner should have them begging for mercy!)

1 The Spanish had a nickname for Francis Drake, 'El Draco'. Draco sounds like Drake, but what does 'El Draco' mean?

a) The dragon.
b) The pirate.
c) Red-beard.

2 Queen Elizabeth gave nicknames to all her close friends. Some were kind but some were cruel. What did she call the French Duke of Anjou who proposed marriage to her?
a) Ou la la.
b) Big Al.
c) Frog.

3 Henry VIII wanted to make an example of the religious rebels in 1537. He had them hanged in a special place. Where?

a) In the Tower of London so the whole city could see them.

b) In their gardens so their wives and children could see them.

c) From the masts of ships so they could tour the country and be seen in every port.

WINDY, ISN'T IT

4 Anne Boleyn rode through London on her way to be crowned queen. Few people cheered and some even booed the unpopular queen. But what did the teenage apprentice lads do?

a) Whistled at Anne as she rode past.

b) Laughed, 'HA! HA!'

c) Sang, God Save the Queen!

5 One of Elizabeth's courtiers wore a new jerkin with tassels. She said, cruelly, 'Your mind is like your jerkin — gone to rags.' The poor man tried to explain they weren't ragged edges but tassels. What did Queen Liz do next?

a) Cut his tassels off with a knife.

b) Had a copy made for herself.

c) Spat on his new jerkin.

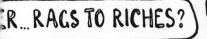

ER... RAGS TO RICHES?

6 Henry VII sent the Earl of Warwick to the scaffold for plotting against him. In fact the Earl was not too bright. What did the Earl do on the short walk from his prison to the scaffold?

a) Got lost.

b) Tried to run away.

c) Snatched a guard's dagger and stabbed himself to death.

HE TRIED TO RUN AWAY BUT HE GOT LOST, SO HE STABBED HIMSELF

7 Henry VIII died on the morning of 28 January 1547. For the next three days what curious thing happened?

a) One by one his faithful dogs died of broken hearts.

b) Henry had all his meals served as usual.

c) The money that he kept in his room disappeared mysteriously.

8 In 1553, Lady Jane Grey was walking through a building that had once been a monastery (until Henry VIII closed it). Suddenly a bloodstained hand shot out through a gap in the wall waving an axe dripping with blood. What was it?

a) The ghost of a murdered monk who wanted revenge on the Tudor Lady.

b) Lady Jane had walked in on a cookery class for the monks.

c) A mad monk wanted to scare the Tudor away.

9 Lady Jane Grey's father, the Earl of Suffolk, was beheaded. What happened to his head?

a) It was preserved and put on display for 400 years.

b) Suffolk was pardoned so the head was sewn back on and he was buried.

c) It was stuck on a pike and displayed over London Bridge.

10 Henry VIII was famous as a great sportsman. But one sporting activity nearly killed him. Was it...?

a) A long jump.

b) A pole vault.

c) A javelin.

Answers

1a 'El Draco' means 'the dragon' and Drake was a monster to the Spanish. Of course he did not have scales, wings or claws and he only breathed fire when he set his beard on fire in mistake for his pipe.

2c She called the Frenchman 'Frog' because the French, even then, were famous for eating frogs' legs.

ZISS IZ VRY STRARNGE, NO? ZEE ENGLISH EAT DRUMSTICKS, BUT DO WE CALL ZEM CHICKENS?

3b That's pretty nasty isn't it? It's not enough that your poor old dad has been executed. But he's left swinging in your back garden so he gets in the way when you want a game of football with your friends.

4b Special arches were placed over the road and decorated with crimson banners. Written in white letters were Henry and Anne's initials. H-A. The apprentice boys pointed at them and went 'HA! HA!' If Henry had any sense he'd have married someone called Isobel-Philippa ... and they'd have been cheered all the way!

5c Her Majesty walked up to the man and spat on the new clothes. He was so ashamed he left the court and never returned. Her ladies-in-waiting were terrified that their dresses would be too fine. The jealous Queen hated that.

6a The Earl of Warwick was said not to know 'a goose from a chicken'. He wandered out of his prison and headed in the wrong direction because he didn't seem to understand that the scaffold over there was for him. Two guards herded him back and the pathetic young man died. He was not clever enough to plot against Henry VII. But, as long as he lived, there would be supporters who might raise an army to set him free. Henry probably invented the 'plot' charge so Warwick's death was murder, really. Not unusual for a Tudor monarch.

7b Henry's death meant the country was without a leader until young Edward's protector could sort things out. Enemies could have attacked while England was leaderless. So foreign visitors were told, 'King Henry VIII is a little poorly but he's still eating well.' Then Henry's meals were carried up to his room with an escort of blasting trumpets. Not even the loudest trumpets would wake the old corpse and it's for certain he didn't enjoy those meals! (But his hounds probably did.)

I HOPE THE PROTECTOR GETS HIS ACT TOGETHER SOON. I DON'T THINK I COULD EAT ANOTHER BEAN

8c An avenging monk wanted to scare the Tudor Lady away from the old building. A bloodstained axe would be enough to scare the spots off a giraffe, but Lady Jane Grey didn't run. The really strange thing is that just a few months later Lady Jane was beheaded with an axe, stained with the blood of her husband. Creepy, eh?

9a His head fell into sawdust steeped in 'tannin' – that's the stuff that turns animal skins into leather. Suffolk's head was preserved like leather and was put on show until the 1940s. It was finally buried in London – about a mile away from his 400-year-dead body. That second grave must have been quite a small one, but the family still put up a headstone. (Head stone, geddit?)

10b In 1525 Henry went out hunting with his hawks. He carried a pole with him and used it to vault across ditches in the countryside. He ran at one ditch, planted the pole in the bottom and vaulted across … when the pole snapped because he was so heavy. He landed head-first in the mud and was stuck so fast he began to choke. A footman grabbed the royal ankles and pulled him to safety. No one laughed – they wouldn't dare – and no one called him an old stick-in-the-mud!

Epilogue

The Tudors came in with a charge of knights and flashing swords at the Battle of Bosworth Field. It was the last such charge in the history of England.

They went out with another great charge but it was the charge of a single horseman.

1485

1603

Queen Elizabeth I took too long to die. She became feeble and lost all the Tudor energy that had driven England for over 100 years. The country was like a car running out of petrol, slowly coasting to a stop. No one cared. Even the servants in her last palace at Richmond left the place filthy and uncared for.

WE LIVE LIKE RATS IN A PALACE

WE *ARE* RATS IN A PALACE

Then, on the night of 23 March 1603, the Queen's lady-in-waiting, Philadelphia Scrope, crossed to a palace window and opened it. She slipped a sapphire ring off her finger and passed it out to her brother, Sir Robert Carey. It was the signal he'd been waiting for. A signal that the last Tudor was dead.

Even though Philadelphia and Robert were the Queen's cousins they weren't going to hang around and weep for the dead woman. They were going to make their fortune by being part of the future. Robert jumped on to the first of a string of fast horses he had arranged along the road north. He galloped through the city, past the carts loaded with victims of the latest plague, and out of the city.

By evening he was in Doncaster. Just 60 hours after leaving London he clattered into Edinburgh. He was bloodied from a fall on the road through the Borders, but King James VI of Scotland welcomed him and heard the news he'd been waiting for. 'Elizabeth is dead. You are named as the next king.'

The days of Tudor terror were over as the slimy Stuarts took over. That's another story for another book. But history is always like that. No sooner has the old died than the new takes over. The old are remembered and preserved in history books.

Some of the 'old' are remembered fondly. Henry VIII is remembered as a strong ruler and Elizabeth has been called the Queen of a 'golden age'. The pain and the misery they caused are often forgotten. To see the past clearly you don't just need history – you need horrible history.

Terrifying Tudors

Quiz

Quick questions

This was the age when the Tudor family brought terror to Britain. Brit sailors discovered new worlds and new ways to kill themselves – like tobacco – while Tudor Tower torturers found new ways to make you suffer. Even queenly necks were on the block while Henry's fat bum was on the throne.

1 In 1502 King James IV of Scotland fell in love with Margaret Drummond, but she died suddenly. What curious thing happened to her sister at the same time? (Clue: double trouble)

2 Henry VIII came to the throne in 1509. Two people had to die so he could become king. Who? (Clue: father and son)

3 In the 1514 Battle of Flodden between England and Scotland, the Earl of Surrey was carried into battle. Why? (Clue: no zimmer frames)

4 Queen Catherine was in charge of England when her army beat the Scots at Flodden because Henry VIII was in France. The Scottish king was hacked down. What gruesome gift did Catherine send Henry to celebrate the win? (Clue: James would be chilly without it)

5 In 1528 the Protestant Scottish rebel Patrick Hamilton was executed. Why was the damp weather bad news for poor Pat? (Clue: smoking is bad for your health)

6 In 1532 a cook, Richard Rosse, poisoned 17 people with his soup. He should have been hanged but Henry VIII thought of a more suitable way to execute a killer cook. What? (Clue: one for the pot)

7 In 1534 a fortune teller, the Holy Maid of Kent, said that Henry VIII would 'die a villain's death' if he married Anne Boleyn. Henry made sure that the Maid died a villain's death. How? (Clue: knot good)

8 In 1535 Henry's friend Thomas More was beheaded for opposing the king. Thomas warned the executioner about his neck. He said, 'Be careful because it's…' What? (Clue: no giraffe)

9 In 1536 Catherine of Aragon died and she was buried in a plain grave. But in Victorian times a group of ladies clubbed together to buy her a marble gravestone. What did they have in common with the dead queen? (Clue: not called Aragon)

10 In 1536 Queen Anne Boleyn was beheaded but not a drop of blood was spilled on the block? Why not? (Clue: someone swipes Anne's head!)

11 On 4 January 1540 Henry VIII was due to marry wife no. 4, Anne of Cleves, but he put it off for two days. Why? (Clue: you might do this with homework!)

12 In 1541 Henry headed off to York to meet the Scottish king, James V. What did James do that made Henry furious? (Clue: stand up?)

13 In 1541 the old Countess of Pole went to the block simply because her son was Henry's enemy. Her behaviour was unusual. How? (Clue: catch me if you can)

14 In 1542 Henry had wife no. 5, Catherine Howard, executed for having boyfriends while she was married to him. He also executed Lady Rochford, Cathy's housekeeper. For what? (Clue: Cupid?)

15 In 1545 Henry VIII went to watch his magnificent warship, the Mary Rose, set sail to sort out the French. What did Mary Rose do to surprise the king? (Clue: behaves in a fishy manner)

16 In September 1546 Henry VIII was very ill. His doctors knew he was dying but they didn't tell him. Why not? (Clue: look what happened to the Holy Maid of Kent)

17 Henry VIII had his dinner delivered to his sick room on 31 January 1547, as he had done for the past month. What was so odd about this delivery? (Clue: he had no appetite)

18 Henry was buried in his huge coffin. There is a gruesome story that Catholic daughter Mary had his corpse dug up. Then what? (Clue: the first of many)

19 Edward VI came to the throne in 1547. Ed's pet dog warned him of a mysterious night-time visitor. What happened to the hero mutt? (Clue: it was a shot in the dark)

Awful Aztecs

In 1519 the Spaniards arrived in Mexico and met the Aztecs. These people made the Tudors look like harmless hamsters. Apart from their horrible habit of human sacrifice, how much do you know about the Aztecs? Answer true or false.

1 Aztec warriors wore metal armour.

2 Aztec princes cut out the hearts of sacrifice victims with a glass knife.

3 Boys were trained to be warriors and were given battle dress when they were still babies.

4 Aztec warriors believed they would become hummingbirds if they died in battle.

5 The Aztecs had public toilets.

6 Warriors with long hair were seen as the best fighters.

7 Aztecs liked to eat scum.

8 An Aztec boy had to ask his best friend for permission to get married.

9 Young Aztec men could be made full warriors by having their faces smeared with the blood of a heart that was still beating.

10 The Spanish caught terrible diseases from the Aztec people.

227

Answers

Quick Tudor quiz

1 Margaret's sister died at the same time. It's a fair bet they were both poisoned. James went on to marry Henry VIII's sister instead.

2 Henry VII (who died in 1509) and also his eldest son, Arthur (who died in 1502).

3 He was 70. The oldest Scot in battle, William Maitland, actually fought and died, and he was 90!

4 Catherine sent the bloodstained coat from the dead King of Scotland. Henry was furious. He wanted the glory of the victory for himself. There's no pleasing some people.

5 Patrick Hamilton was burned to death but the damp weather meant he burnt slowly. The executioners tried to put gunpowder on the fire but that only scorched him.

6 Henry ordered that Rosse be boiled alive in his own pot. Rosse always said that he put the poison in the pot as a joke – it wasn't meant to kill.

7 She was hanged along with three men who supported her attack on the king.

8 Very short. He asked the executioner to try and be an accurate shot with the axe.

9 They were all called 'Catherine'.

10 Anne wasn't beheaded on a block. She knelt down and her head was removed with a single swipe of a sword. It was said her lips kept moving in prayer for minutes after her head was off.

11 Henry tried to put it off until he could find an excuse not to do it. He didn't want to marry Anne after all, but he knew if he refused he would upset her powerful father. In the end he had to go ahead.

12 James didn't turn up. James's councillors said Henry was planning a trap.

13 She moved her head around to make the job as difficult as possible for the executioner.

It took him several chops at her shoulders before he finally hit her neck and got her head off.

14 Lady Rochford arranged the meetings between Catherine and her boyfriends.

15 Rolled over and sank. It may have been top heavy with guns and men and the boat was upset. Henry was upset too – but 500 people on board were dead upset. Simply dead, in fact.

16 It was illegal for anyone to say, 'The king is going to die.' So they didn't say it – but he died anyway.

17 Henry had died three days earlier on 28 January. The lords wanted his death kept secret for a few days till the throne was safe for Edward VI to take it. They had meals delivered to the room to make it seem normal. But who ate them?

18 She had him burned. Probably not true.

19 The dog was shot dead by the visitor, who was Ed's uncle. He was executed, and the mutt was avenged.

Awful Aztecs

1 False. They had armour but it was made of hardened cotton.

2 True. The knives were made from a type of natural glass called 'obsidian'.

3 True. They were given a loincloth, shield, cloak and four arrows when they were a few days old.

4 True. They believed they would hum off to join the Sun God.

5 True. And the human manure would be used as fertilizer for crops.

6 False. Warriors couldn't get their hair cut until they'd killed someone in battle.

7 True. Lake scum was made into cakes.

8 False. He had to ask his teacher!

9 True.

10 False. The Spanish brought diseases from Europe which killed many Aztecs.

Interesting Index

COLLECT THE WHOLE HORRIBLE LOT!